1/5/85

To my "sister" –
the one I always
wanted and never
had til' you!

My prayers are with
you tomorrow and may
your recovery be fast.

Love,
Carenne

TO CHEER YOU

Get Well Wishes
and
Sunny Thoughts

The C. R. Gibson Company, Norwalk, Connecticut

This book of happy thoughts
comes with many get-well wishes.

THE DAY

The day will bring some lovely thing,
I say it over each new dawn;
"Some gay, adventurous thing to hold
Against my heart, when it is gone."
And so I rise and go to meet
The day with wings upon my feet.

I come upon it unaware—
Some sudden beauty without name;
A snatch of song, a breath of pine;
A poem lit with golden flame;
High tangled bird notes, keenly thinned,
Like flying color on the wing.

No day has ever failed me quite—
Before the grayest day is done,
I come upon some misty bloom
Or a late line of crimson sun.
Each night I pause, remembering
Some gay, adventurous, lovely thing.

—Grace Noll Crowell

WONDERS OF THE WORLD

Look for the stars, you'll say there are none;
Look up a second time, and, one by one,
You mark them twinkling out with silvery light,
And wonder how they could elude the sight!
                                    —William Wordsworth

The beauty of the world and
the orderly arrangement of
everything celestial makes us
confess that there is an excel-
lent and eternal nature, which
ought to be worshipped and
admired by all mankind.
                                    —Cicero

If the stars should appear one
night in a thousand years, how
would men believe and adore!
                                    —Ralph Waldo Emerson

I forget how many thousand eggs go wrong for one codfish that gets hatched. But as Berkeley said long ago, it is idle to censure the creation as wasteful if you believe in a creator who has unlimited stuff to play with. And anyway, why be sorry for the things we don't miss?

—Sir Frederick Pollock

Every moment of this strange and lovely life from dawn to dusk is a miracle. Somewhere, always, a rose is opening its petals to the dawn. Somewhere, always, a flower is fading in the dusk. The incense that rises with the sun, and the scents that die in the dark, are all gathered, sooner or later, into the solitary fragrance that is God. Faintly, elusively that fragrance lingers over all of us.

—Beverly Nichols

REJOICE

*. . . The finches sing my thoughts away.
I feel so happy, so green and so full of
shoots. Over my head sits a little bird
with beautifully shiny feathers, soulful
eyes and vibrancy in his voice.*

*"Take spring when it comes, and rejoice
. . . Take happiness when it comes, and
rejoice . . . Take love when it comes, and
rejoice . . ."*

*The sun shines, the anemones nod in
the wind. The trees are budding while
the worms burrow and the earth is full
of eggs and seeds.*

—Carl Ewald

ONLY THE WIND SAYS SPRING

The grass still is pale, and spring is yet only a
  wind stirring
    Over the open field.
There is no green even under the forest leaves.
    No buds are blurring
    The pencil sketch of trees. No meadows yield
The song of larks, nor the buzz of bees conferring.
Only the wind says spring. Everything else
  shouts winter:
    The whitened beards of grass,
The shriveled legs of corn with their trousers
  flapping,
    The year-old cuts in the root of the sassafras;
A spruce-cone empty of seeds, the scales
  unwrapping
    Open to dryness, last year's withered peach,
A stiff tomato-vine begun to splinter,
    The crones of milkweed talking each to each.

The earth stands mute, without a voice to sing.
But the wind is saying spring.

                        —Helen Janet Miller

STARS

Alone in the night
    On a dark hill
With pines around me
    Spicy and still,

And a heaven full of stars
    Over my head,
White and topaz
    And misty red;

Myriads with beating
    Hearts of fire
That aeons
    Cannot vex or tire;

Up the dome of heaven
    Like a great hill,
I watch them marching
    Stately and still,

And I know that I
    Am honored to be
Witness
    Of so much majesty.

—Sara Teasdale

GIFTS

A contributing factor to happiness is to be able to enjoy the gifts of nature. The poorest man living can enjoy these, for such blessings are free. Everybody can take pleasure in a glorious sunset. You would have to pay a great sum for a painting by a skilled artist. Only the wealthy can afford it, but almost any evening we can look at a brilliant western sky, and each one of us can say, "That's mine!"

—David O. McKay

*To some people a tree is some-
thing so incredibly beautiful
that it brings tears to the eyes.
To others it is just a green
thing that stands in the way.*

—William Blake

FRIENDSHIP IS GOLDEN

Life is to be fortified by many friend-ships. To love and to be loved is the greatest happiness of existence.

—Sydney Smith

It is a mistake to think that one makes a friend because of his or her qualities; it has nothing to do with qualities at all. It is the person that we want, not what he does or says, or does not do or say, but what he is! that is eternally enough.

—Arthur Christopher Benson

There is in friendship some-
thing of all relations, and some-
thing above them all. It is the
golden thread that ties the
hearts of all hearts of all the
world.

—John Evelyn

My friends are my estate. For-
give me then the avarice to
hoard them!

—Emily Dickinson

Indeed, we do not really live
unless we have friends sur-
rounding us like a firm wall
against the winds of the world.

—Charles Hanson Towne

THE BEST GIFTS

In gratitude for God's gift of life to us we should share that gift with others. The art of giving encompasses many areas. It is an outgoing, overflowing way of life.

Basically we give what we are. "The thoughts you think," wrote Maeterlinck, "will irradiate you as though you are a transparent vase."

The gifts of things are never as precious as the gifts of thought.

Emerson said it well: "Rings and jewels are not gifts, but apologies for gifts. The only true gift is a portion of thyself."

We give of ourselves when we give gifts of the heart: love, kindness, joy, understanding, sympathy, tolerance, forgiveness.

We give of ourselves when we give gifts of the mind: ideas, dreams, purposes, ideals, principles, plans, inventions, projects, poetry.

We give of ourselves when we give gifts of the spirit: prayer, vision, beauty, aspiration, peace, faith.

We give of ourselves when we give the gift of time: when we are minute builders of more abundant living for others.

We give of ourselves when we give the gift of words: encouragement, inspiration, guidance.

—Wilferd A. Peterson

LOVE, THE UNIVERSAL LANGUAGE

*We need to love and to be loved as much
as we need bread or water or a roof. With-
out it we are not happy, we only exist. The
two outstanding themes of history have
been freedom and love.*

—F. Alexander Magoun

*One must not be mean with
affections; what is spent of the
funds is renewed in the spend-
ing itself. Left untouched for
too long, they diminish imper-
ceptibly or the lock gets rusty;
they are there all right but one
cannot make use of them.*

—Sigmund Freud

Light breaks where no sun
  shines;
Where no sea runs, the waters
  of the heart
Push in their tides.

—Dylan Thomas

Love fulfills our need to be
sympathetically understood by
someone to whom we can pour
out our troubles, by whom we
can be comforted, with whom
we can go on to find gladness.
It is a relationship forever re-
newed . . . an emotional close-
ness which prevents a person
from feeling alone inside.

—F. Alexander Magoun

LOVE IS . . .

Nothing is sweeter than love, nothing more courageous, nothing higher, nothing wider, nothing more pleasant, nothing fuller nor better in Heaven and earth, because love is born of God, and cannot rest but in God, above all created things. Love feels no burden, thinks nothing of trouble, attempts what is above its strength, pleads no excuse of impossibility . . . It is therefore able to undertake all things, and it completes many things, and warrants them to take effect,

where he who does not love would faint and lie down. Love is watchful and sleeping, slumbereth not. Though weary, it is not tired; though pressed, it is not straitened; though alarmed, it is not confounded; but, as a lively flame and burning torch, it forces its way upwards and securely passes all.

—Thomas á Kempis

HAPPINESS GLOWS

*Happiness is a sunbeam which
may pass through a thousand
bosoms without losing a par-
ticle of its original ray; nay,
when it strikes a kindred heart,
like the converged light upon
a mirror, it reflects itself with
redoubled brightness.—It is not
perfected till it is shared.*

—Jane Porter

*May we never let the things
we can't have, or don't have,
or shouldn't have, spoil our en-
joyment of the things we do
have and can have. As we value
our happiness let us not forget
it, for one of the greatest les-
sons in life is learning to be
happy without the things we
cannot or should not have.*

—Richard L. Evans

The art of being happy lies in the power of extracting happiness from common things.

—Henry Ward Beecher

I have had a happy life, and there is not much of it I would change if I could live it over again . . . . I would gladly chant a paen for the world as I find it. What a mighty interesting place to live in!

—John Burroughs

As yesterday is history, and tomorrow may never come, I have resolved that from this day on, I will do all the business I can honestly, have all the fun I can reasonably, do all the good I can willingly, and save my digestion by thinking pleasantly.

—Robert Louis Stevenson

WEAR A HAPPY FACE

In this art of being happy which I am pro-
posing, I should also include some practical
advice about making good use of bad
weather. At the moment I am writing this,
it is raining; there is a patter on the roof;
hundreds of little rills are chattering; the
air is clean, almost filtered; the storm clouds
are like strips of magnificent cloth. One
must learn to seize such beauties. "But,"
someone says, "rain ruins the harvest." An-
other complains: "Mud makes everything
dirty." And still a third: "It's so nice to be
able to sit on the grass." Of course, every-
one feels the same way; but your complain-
ing does no good; and I get inundated with
complaints that follow me even into my own
home. Especially in rainy weather one wants
to see smiling faces. So, show a happy face
in bad weather.

—Alain

HAPPINESS IS A SIMPLE THING

The whole subject of happiness has, in my opinion, been treated too solemnly. It has been thought that men cannot be happy without a "theory of life." Actually, it is the simple things that really matter. If a man delights in his wife and children, has success in work, and finds pleasure in the alternation of day and night, spring and autumn, he will be happy whatever his philosophy may be.

—Bertrand Russell

LAUGHTER IS GOD'S GIFT

. . . among those things I believe in most is laughter. This is a sad world . . . . But even in my darkest moments, abandoned seemingly by all, I found that I was always saved if I could laugh. Laughter breaks evil spells, changes luck. Laughter is on the side of God.

—George Anthiel

Seek out every opportunity for laughter that you can, for laughter is one of those things, like music and flowers, that God has given us to relieve the tensions that we undergo in this life.

—Preston Bradley

Mirth is the sweet wine of human life. It should be offered sparkling with zestful life unto God.

—Henry Ward Beecher

If your everyday life seems poor to you, do not accuse it; accuse yourself, tell yourself you are not poet enough to summon up its riches; since for the Creator there is no poverty and no poor or unimportant place.

—Rainer Maria Rilke

Gladness of heart is the very life of man, cheerfulness prolongs his days.

—Ecclesiasticus 30:22

"There is a time to weep, and a time to laugh," says Ecclesiastes. This Old Testament writer . . . contended that "for everything there is a season." I am glad he included laughter. Religious people ought to remember that laughter is as much a part of God's order as is prayer . . . .

Genuine laughter—not the bitter, cynical wisecrack or the vulgarity which is a substitute for real humor—arises out of a sense of well-being. Such a sense can come only from confidence in the ultimate trustworthiness of life . . . .

There is much cause for sorrow in this world. But there is also a time to laugh.

—L. D. Johnson

LIVING FOR TODAY

*If we are ever to enjoy life, now is the time—
not tomorrow, nor next year, nor in some
future life. The best preparation for a better
life next year is a full, complete, harmonious,
joyous life this year. Our beliefs in a rich
future life are of little importance unless we
coin them into a rich pleasant life. Today
should always be our most wonderful day.*

—Thomas Dreier

*It is good for one to appreciate that life is
now. Whatever it offers, little or much, life
is now—this day—this hour—and is probably
the only experience of the kind one is to
have. As the doctor said to the woman who
complained that she did not like the night
air: "Madam, during certain hours of the
twenty-four, night air is the only air there
is."*

—Charles Macomb Flandrau

Remember when old December's darkness is all about you, that the world is really in every minute and point as full of life as in the most joyous morning you ever lived.

—William James

I have tried too in my time to be a philosopher; but I don't know how, cheerfulness was always breaking in.

—Oliver Edwards

I have only one life, and it is short enough. Why waste it on things I don't want most?

—Louis Brandeis

A MINUTE IS A MIRACLE

I believe that only one person in a thousand knows the trick of really living in the present. Most of us spend 59 minutes an hour living in the past, with regret for lost joys, or shame for things badly done (both utterly useless and weakening)—or in a future which we either long for or dread. Yet the past is gone beyond prayer, and every minute you spend in the vain effort to anticipate the future is a moment lost. There is only one world, the world pressing against you at this minute. There is only one minute in which you are alive, this minute—here and now. *The only way to live is by accepting each minute as an unrepeatable miracle. Which is exactly what it is—a miracle and unrepeatable.*

—Storm Jameson

LEARNING FROM LIFE

A fresh mind keeps the body fresh. Take in the ideas of the day, drain off those of yesterday. As to the morrow, time enough to consider it when it becomes today.
—Edward George Bulwer-Lytton

An open mind is all very well in its way, but it ought not to be so open that there is no keeping anything in or out of it. It should be capable of shutting its doors sometimes, or it may be found a little draughty.
—Samuel Butler

Think! I've got enough to do, and little enough to get for it, without thinking.
—Charles Dickens

Wisdom is born of experience, sometimes hard experience. The point is to learn the lesson, gain new insight, get a sounder perspective.

—F. Alexander Magoun

What you are doing is, of course, in the first place, living. And life involves passions, faiths, doubts and courage. The critical inquiry into what these things mean and imply is philosophy.

—Josiah Royce

What a blessing it would be if we could open and shut our ears as easily as we do our eyes.

—G. C. Lichtenberg

Noise proves nothing. Often a hen who has merely laid an egg cackles as if she had laid an asteroid.

—Mark Twain

CUP OF HAPPINESS

Lord God, how full our cup of happiness!
We drink and drink—and yet it grows not less;
But every morn the newly risen sun
Finds it replenished, sparkling, over-run!
Hast Thou not given us raiment, warmth, and meat,
And in due season all earth's fruits to eat?
Work for our hands and rainbows for our eyes,
And for our souls the wings of butterflies?

A father's smile, a mother's fond embrace,
The tender light upon a lover's face?
The talk of friends, the twinkling eye of mirth,
The whispering silence of the good green earth?
Hope for our youth, and memories for age,
And psalms upon the heavens' moving page?
And dost Thou not of pain a mingling pour
To make the cup but overflow the more?

—Gilbert Thomas

SOUND ADVICE

*I forget who it was that recommended men
for their soul's good to do each day two
things they disliked . . . it is a precept that
I have followed scrupulously; for every day
I have got up and I have gone to bed.*
                                    —W. Somerset Maugham

*If you have occasional spells of despondency
and self-pity, if once in a while you begin
to feel sorry for yourself, don't despair! The
sun has a sinking spell every night, but it
rises again all right the next morning.*
                                    —Richard C. Hertz

*The only way to keep your health is to eat
what you don't want, drink what you don't
like and do what you'd rather not.*
                                    —Mark Twain

The crab, more than any of God's creatures, has formulated the perfect philosophy of life. Whenever he is confronted by a great moral crisis in life, he first makes up his mind what is right, and then goes sideways as fast as he can.

—Oliver Herford

As for exercise, if you have to take it, take it and put up with it. But as long as you have the price of a hack and can hire other people to play baseball for you and run races and do gymnastics when you sit in the shade and smoke and watch them—great heavens, what more do you want?

—Stephen Leacock

The best way to get real enjoyment out of a garden is to put on a wide straw hat, dress in thin, loose-fitting clothes, hold a trowel in one hand and a cold drink in the other, and tell the man where to dig.

—Charles Barr

. . .DAWNING. . .DAWNING

Stand high upon a mountain,
*   as day is born anew . . .*
Kneel down and smell a flower,
*   still fresh with morning dew . . .*
Run beside the river,
*   so wild, and free, and blue,*
Reach out your hand,
*   and catch the wind,*
*   it will not wait for you . . .*
Walk slowly through the meadow,
*   till closing of the day . . .*
Reach out and touch the sunset,
*   before it slips away.*

—Nell Herring

A TIME TO RELAX

*A hobby is something a man does, not be-
cause he thinks he should or because some-
one else wants him to, but because he likes
doing it . . . . You don't have to do it well
for it to be a hobby. You only have to
enjoy it.*

—Hannah Lees

*No man is really happy or safe without a
hobby, and it makes precious little differ-
ence what the outside interest may be—
botany, beetles or butterflies, roses, tulips
or irises; fishing, mountaineering or an-
tiques—anything will do so long as he strad-
dles a hobby and rides it hard.*

—Sir William Osler

*I can't quite explain it, but I
don't believe one can ever be
unhappy for long provided one
does just exactly what one
wants to and when one wants
to.*

—Evelyn Waugh

Talking of pleasure, this moment I was writing with one hand, and with the other holding to my mouth a nectarine. Good God, how fine! It went down soft, pulpy, slushy, oozy—all its delicious embonpoint melted down my throat like a large beatified strawberry.

—John Keats

"The love of routine," a scientific friend said to me once, "is nothing to be ashamed of. It is only the love of knowing how to do things which nature plants in every child, kitten, and puppy."

—Joyce Cary

He does not seem to me to be a free man who does not sometimes do nothing.

—Cicero

He who can no longer pause to wonder and stand rapt in awe is as good as dead; his eyes are closed.

—Albert Einstein

SPRING CALLED ME

Spring called me from my work today
To climb a far-off hill.
Because I heard a robin sing
And saw each daffodil,
My mind just wandered off, it seemed
My heart was far away,
And quickly I was off and gone
Where little streamlets play.

Spring put a song within my heart
And laughter in my eyes;
For spring held naught but wondrous joy
And pleasant sweet surprise.
I picked a smiling violet
And loved its gentle charms,
I saw a precious nesting bird
Within the oak tree's arms.

Spring called me from my work today
And taught me how to dream,
And left me in a happy mood
Beside a laughing stream.
I loved this early April morn,
The blue skies overhead . . .
When springtime called me from my work
And bid me play instead.

—Garnett Ann Schultz

SO MUCH TO APPRECIATE

The deepest principle of human nature is the craving to be appreciated.

—William James

A habit for all of us to develop would be to look for something to appreciate in everyone we meet. We can all be generous with appreciation. Everyone is grateful for it. It improves every human relationship, it brings new courage to people facing difficulties, and it brings out the best in everyone. So, give appreciation generously whenever you can. You will never regret it.

—Carl Holmes

It is a great mistake for men to give up paying compliments, for when they give up saying what is charming, they give up thinking what is charming.

—Oscar Wilde

We crave the companionship of those who can understand, and long for the presence of one who sympathizes with our aspirations, comprehends our hopes and is able to partake of our joys . . . . Thoughts materialize into deeds only when Some One vitalizes by approval. Every good thing is loved into life.

—Elbert Hubbard

Look for the best in everything, like the bee which finds honey in the thorniest plants. Applaud the achievements of others; if you find faults, treat them with kindliness and understanding. The generous-minded finds one beauty in a thousand defects; the small-minded one defect in a thousand beauties.

—Baltasar Gracian

Blossoms are scattered by the wind and the wind cares nothing, but the blossoms of the heart no wind can touch.

—Yoshida Kenkō

WELLSPRINGS OF LIFE

We have a new awareness today of what it means to be human, perhaps because "human-ness" is threatened. I had a sense of this human essence as I watched the first moon walk. I did not feel it in the miraculous landing itself; nor in Armstrong's breathtaking, cautious first step off the ladder, nor in the slow, methodical mo-tions of those two men, muffled and padded in space suits, as they set up their equipment. It came to me the moment when, having gained their "moon legs," they began to leap, to bounce lightly over the surface of the moon like bal-loons, in an expansive moment of play—unnec-essary play (even though programmed into the schedule of work). In those few instants I felt, with relief, what it is to be human. Play, joy, spontaneity—these are the wellsprings of crea-tivity. They may be extras but they are among the most marvelous attributes of man. We can-not abandon them and still be fully human.

—Anne Morrow Lindbergh

PEOPLE NEED PEOPLE

*There are two statements about human
beings that are true: that all human beings
are alike, and that all are different. On
those two facts all human wisdom is founded.*

—Mark Van Doren

*We forget that there is no hope
of joy except in human rela-
tions. If I summon up those
memories that have left me
with an enduring savor, if I
draw up the balance sheet of
the hours in my life that have
truly counted, surely I find
only those that no wealth could
have procured me. True riches
cannot be bought.*

—Antoine de Saint-Exupéry

How do we become true and good, happy and genuine, joyful and free? Never by magic, never by chance, never by sitting and waiting, but only by getting in touch with good, true, happy, genuine human beings, only by seeking the company of the strong and the free, only by catching spontaneity and freedom from those who are themselves spontaneous and free.

—Charles Malik

WHEN GOD SENDS A BEAUTIFUL DAY

Somehow the world seems a wonderful place.
There's an excitement that quickens the pace
. . . Suddenly everyone's smiling and gay—
When God sends a beautiful day.

You cannot explain it, you do not know why—
but things look quite different when from the
sky—the sun in its glory from Heaven looks
down—pouring its blessings on country and town.

The troubles that yesterday weighted on your
mind—seem unimportant. You leave them behind
. . . The future looks bright and your cares
melt away—when God sends a beautiful day.

—Patience Strong

ACKNOWLEDGMENTS

The editor and the publisher have made every effort to trace the ownership of all copyrighted material and to secure permission from copyright holders of such material. In the event of any question arising as to the use of any material the publisher and editor, while expressing regret for inadvertent error, will be pleased to make the necessary corrections in future printings. Thanks are due to the following authors, publishers, publications and agents for permission to use the material indicated.

BRANDT AND BRANDT, for excerpt from *Here and Now* by Storm Jameson, reprinted with permission from the August 1956 Reader's Digest. Copyright © 1955 by Storm Jameson.

RUPERT CREW LIMITED, for "When God Sends a Beautiful Day" from *Harvest of a Quiet Eye* by Patience Strong.

EXPOSITION PRESS, INC., for "Only the Wind Says" from *After War and Other Poems* by Helen Janet Miller.

HARCOURT BRACE JOVANOVICH, INC., for excerpt from *Earth Shine* by Anne Morrow Lindbergh, copyright © 1966, 1969 by Anne Morrow Lindbergh; for excerpt from *Wind, Sand and Stars* by Antoine de Saint-Exupery, copyright 1939 by Antoine de Saint-Exupery, renewed 1967 by Lewis Galantiere.

HARPER & ROW, PUBLISHERS, INC., for "The Day" from *Poems of Inspiration and Courage* by Grace Noll Crowell, copyright 1928, 1934 by Harper & Row, Publishers, Inc., renewed 1956, 1962 by Grace Noll Crowell; for excerpts abridged and adapted from *Living a Happy Life* by F. Alexander Magoun copyright © 1960 by F. Alexander Magoun.

HAWTHORN BOOKS, INC., for excerpt from *Help Your Husband Stay Alive* by Hannah Lees, copyright 1957.

NELL HERRING, for "Dawning, Dawning."

HORIZON PRESS, for excerpt by Carl Ewald from *My Little Boy, My Big Girl* by Beth Bolling copyright 1962.

MACMILLAN PUBLISHING CO. INC., for "Stars" from *Collected Poems* by Sara Teasdale, copyright 1920 by Macmillan Publishing Co. Inc., renewed 1948 by Mamie T. Wheless.

GARNETT ANN SCHULTZ for "Spring Called Me."

SIMON & SCHUSTER, INC., for excerpt from *The Art of Living* by Wilferd A. Peterson, copyright 1960, 1961 by Wilferd A. Peterson.

GILBERT THOMAS, for "The Cup of Happiness."

FREDERICK UNGAR PUBLISHING CO. INC., for excerpt from *Alain on Happiness*, copyright © 1973 by Frederick Ungar Publishing Co. Inc.

Selected by Elizabeth Gibson

Set in Colonial italic

Designed by Diane Kane,
    Publishers Graphics

PHOTO CREDITS

*Four By Five, Inc. — p. 2, p. 3, p. 11, p. 22, p. 27, p. 30; Michael
Powers — p. 6; State Development Office of Maine — p. 14, p. 15,
p. 38; Gene Ruestmann — p. 23, p. 43; Stanford Burns — p. 35; Peter
Tepper — p. 39; Jay Johnson — p. 47; Bruce Ando — p. 50; Ray
Mainwaring — p. 55. p. 18.*